Getting along together:
Baby and I can play

Written by
Karen Hendrickson

Illustrated by
Marina Megale

LC 85-60715

ISBN 0-943990-12-2 (paper)
ISBN 0-943990-13-0 (lib. binding)

Copyright © 1985   Karen Hendrickson
Copyright © 1985   Marina Megale

Parenting Press, Inc.
7750 31st Ave. NE
Seattle, WA 98115

Big brothers and sisters are special people who have little brothers and sisters.

This is a book for big brothers and sisters whose little brothers and sisters are babies. It will show you how to play with your baby

and it will tell you what to do when you wish your baby brother or sister would go away.

Babies change as they grow. They like different toys and games at different ages.

Very little babies learn by seeing and hearing people and things close to them. You can help your baby learn by showing her toys and other things you think she might like.

Babies like to watch their big brothers and sisters play. Ask your mom or dad to put the baby in a place where he or she can watch you. You can watch the baby watching you!

Babies like to be cuddled and gently stroked most of the time. Watch your baby's face to be sure she likes the way you touch her.

Your baby will let you know when she wants to touch what you show her by waving her hands. Dangle toys close to her hands while she hits at them. Think of things that will move when your baby hits them: a rag doll, a scarf or a balloon on a very short string.

Talk to your baby often. Talk about what you are doing and what she is doing. Make the sounds she makes and see if she will say them back to you.

At first a baby's hands are closed into tight little fists. When your baby begins holding her hands open more often you can hand her toys and other interesting things to feel, hear or taste. Be sure to talk with your mom and dad about what is safe for the baby.

When your baby figures out how to let go of the things you hand her, she will want you to pick them up for her again and again and again. This can be a fun game for big kids and babies to play together and it's how your baby learns.

About the time that babies are learning to sit, they are old enough for peek-a-boo and other hiding games. Try hiding the baby's toy under a blanket. Let her pull off the blanket to find the toy. Think of other ways that you can play peek-a-boo with your baby.

When babies begin to crawl, they like to play chase games. Try crawling after your little brother or sister and see what happens!

If you clap your hands, wave or throw a kiss does your baby do the same thing? If she does, she is ready for copy-games. Think of some other copy games you can have fun with together.

You and your baby brother or sister can think of other things that are fun to do. Did you do something today that was fun for both of you?

Sometimes it's no fun at all having a baby brother or sister. You might even wish you didn't have a baby. Most big brothers and sisters feel this way at times.

Sometimes it seems like Mom and Dad don't have enough time for you now. One of the hardest things for big kids to do is to share their mom and dad.

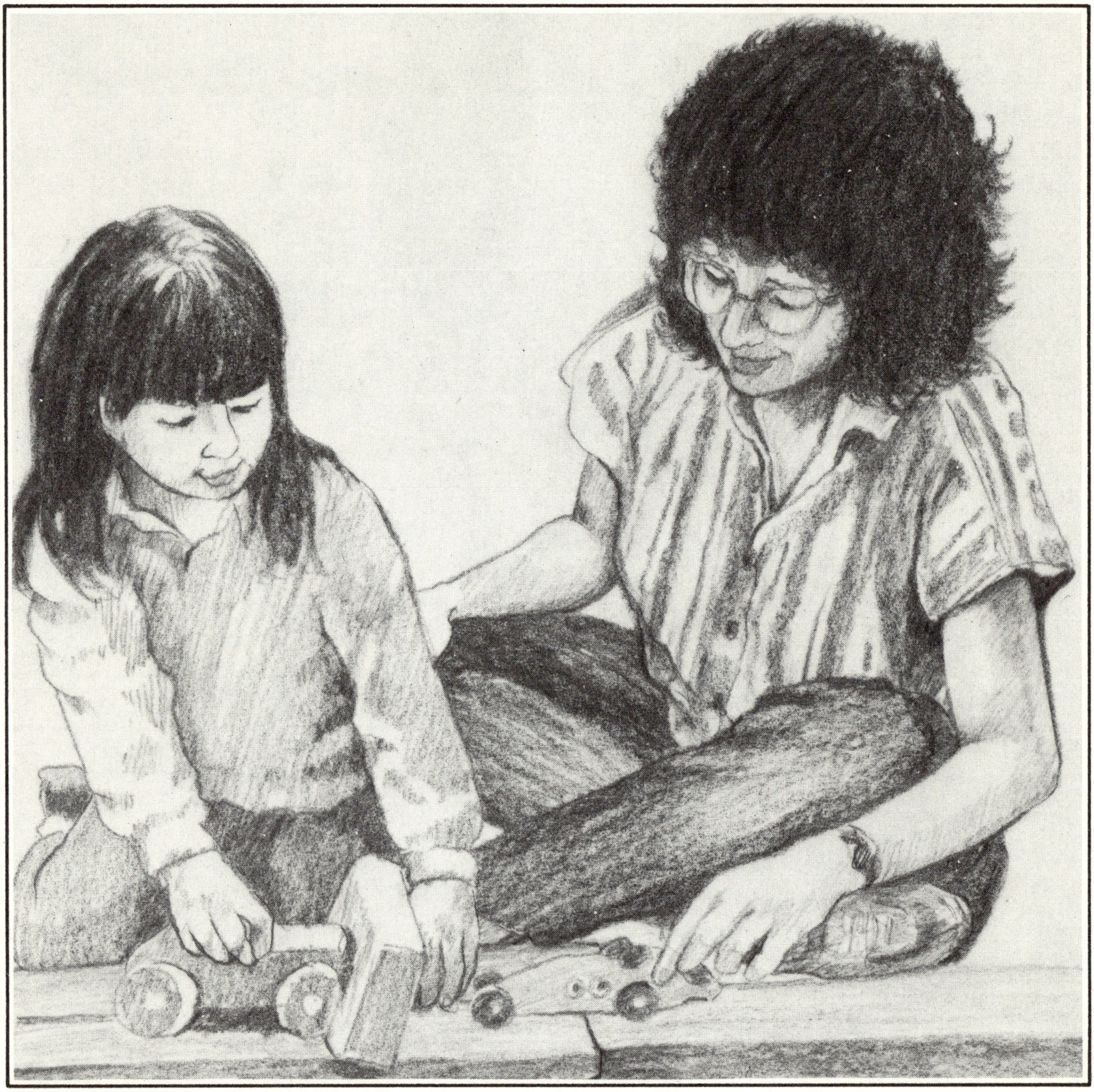

Tell your mom when you need some time alone with her. She can plan a special time for you to be together.

It helps to plan some special things to do when your mom is busy. Some families make a special "nursing box" with games and toys to play with when Mom is feeding the baby.

Babies often use things that belonged to their big brothers and sisters, like cribs, high chairs and toys. Sometimes big brothers and sisters want them back again.

Ask your mom and dad if you can try out the baby's things sometime. You may find that they're not as much fun as you thought. Think of it as taking turns. When you were a baby you had your turn to drink from bottles or breasts and to wear baby clothes. Now it is your baby's turn.

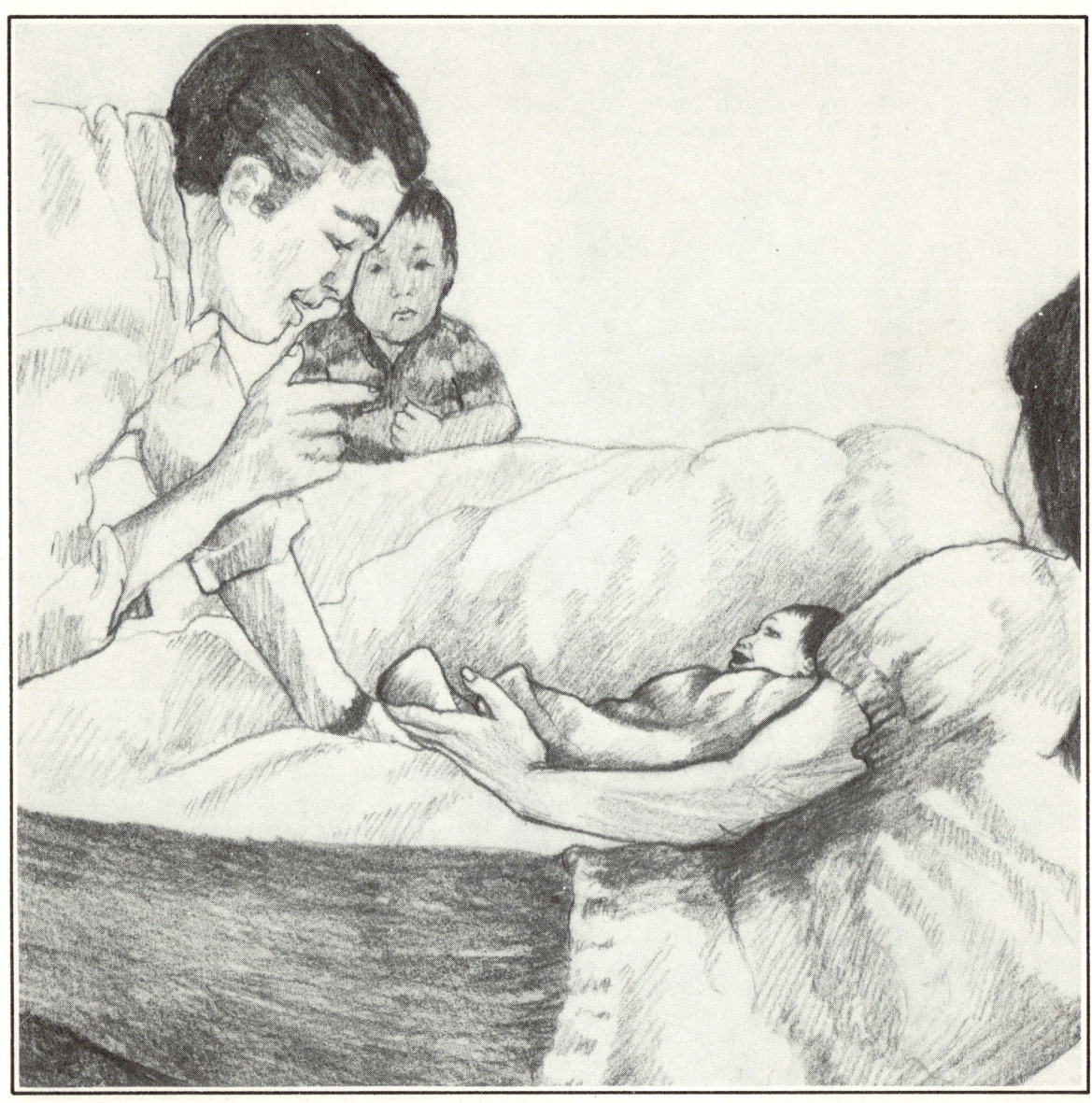

Babies need lots of care while they are little. Sometimes though, older children see all the attention babies get and they worry that maybe their mom or dad loves the baby best. As your baby grows older she will be able to do more and more for herself.

Talk with your mom or dad about how you feel. They will help you to understand how special and important you are to them.

You are also special and important to your baby. What a lucky baby she is to have a brother or sister who knows how to play with a baby!

NOTE TO PARENTS

This book is designed to help children play appropriately with their infant siblings and to feel good about themselves as big brothers and sisters. The first section describes simple activities which children and babies can do together. The second section gives examples of problems commonly experienced by older siblings and suggests solutions.

Children will need help in using these suggestions with their baby brother or sister. You can help your child by talking about the activities as you read the book together and by relating them to the specific needs and temperament of your infant. Encourage your child to expand upon the activities in the book and to contribute his or her own ideas. Additional information and comments are listed for each page. The italicized questions can be used to help your child apply the information directly to his or her family situation.

Page 1: *What ways does (your baby's name) have to show you how special you are to him or her?* The baby might smile, hold onto fingers or watch the older child. Let your child know what a special big brother or sister you think she is.

Page 2: *What do you already know about playing with babies?* Share some of the positive ways that you have seen your child playing with the baby.

Page 3: *Do you sometimes wish (your baby's name) would go away?* Be sure to accept your child's answer here as well as negative feelings expressed about the baby at other times. For example, you could say "It is OK to be mad at the baby, but it is not OK to hit or hurt the baby."

Page 4: *What things can (your baby's name) do right now?* Talk about the new things that your baby is learning to do and the things that she is likely to do soon. For example, your baby may smile, watch people and things, grasp things, make sounds, etc.

Page 5: *What things do you think the baby likes to look at?* Suggest that your child try pictures of faces, pictures of distinctive patterns with contrasting colors or brightly colored toys.

Page 6: *Have you ever noticed (your baby's name) watching you play?* An infant seat enables a very young baby to see more of what is going on around her. Think together about positions that will be safe for the baby and help her to use her eyes.

Page 7: *How does the baby let you know that she likes the way you are touching her?* Although it requires considerably more watchfulness on your part, both the baby and older sibling(s) will benefit if the baby is frequently accessible to her siblings. A blanket, infant seat or mattress placed on the floor can provide this kind of accessibility.

Page 8: *Why do you think the baby likes things that move?* Talk with your child about how good it makes a baby feel to grab something or make it move. Make sure that the objects your child selects are safe for an infant and that any strings are short enough (no longer than 5 inches) that they cannot become wrapped around the baby's neck.

Page 9: *What sounds does (your baby's name) make now?* Suggest that your child repeat a sound that he has heard the baby make, such as "da-da-da", and that he give the baby time to make it back. Place the baby so she can see your child's face as he talks or makes sounds.

Page 10: *What kinds of toys are safe for a baby?* Talk with your child about choosing toys that are too big to fit in the baby's mouth, have no small pieces that might break off and have no sharp or rough edges.

Page 11: *What toys would be fun for (your baby's name) to drop?* Your child might like to try things that make different kinds of sounds as they hit the floor, eg. balls, blocks, metal baby food jar lids or rattles.

Page 12: *What other ways can you play peek-a-boo with (your baby's name)?* Your child can hide himself and jump out calling "Peek-a-boo". Or he can try hiding the baby's eyes with a light blanket which he or the baby removes.

Page 13: *What things do we have to be careful about when the baby is crawling?* Remind your child about stairs (it is best to block stairs with mesh gates when possible) and any other danger spots in your home. She may need a reminder not to put her full weight on the baby if she crawls over her.

Page 14: *What are some other copy games?* Encourage your child to think about things that he knows the baby will be able to do. For example, suggest that the child put his hands over his head, touch his nose, ears, etc.

Page 15: *What are some other ways that you and (your baby's name) can have fun together?* Note the activities that your child has already thought of and done with the baby and praise her for trying those things.

Page 16: *What are some things that you can do when you are angry and upset with (your baby's name)?* Tell your child that it is OK to be angry, even at people you love. Suggest that she do something active, like run around the house three times, make up a mad dance or go off by herself when she feels angry.

Page 17: *When is it hard for you to share your Mom and Dad? What can you do at those times?* Encourage your child to think of things she enjoys doing alone.

Page 18: *What would you like to do during our special time?* Even though time alone with each child can be hard to come by, a daily time alone with Mom or Dad has been shown to be one of the most useful things parents can do to minimize sibling rivalry. Possible "special times" with an older sibling can be planned when the baby is sleeping or being cared for by the other parent or a school-aged sitter.

Page 19: *Would you like to make a nursing box?* You and your child might enjoy pasting pictures, ribbons or lace on a cardboard box to make it a special "nursing box." It should be available only when Mom is feeding the baby. Interest can also be maintained by changing the contents regularly.

Page 20: *What things does the baby use that once belonged to you?* For example, your child might name the crib, baby clothes, bottle, toys, diapers, etc.

Page 21: *Is there something that (your baby's name) uses that you would like to try out sometime?* It is OK for your child to "try on" old behavior occasionally. Older siblings often like to "play baby."

Page 22: *Do you remember when you weren't able to talk or walk and we had to do everything for you?* Your child probably does not remember but most kids love hearing about themselves as babies or seeing pictures. This kind of reminiscing helps kids to understand that babies get extra care and attention because they require it, not because they are more special to their parents.

Page 23: *What are some good times for talking to Mom and Dad about how you feel? How can you let us know when you need to talk about something right away?* It is important that parents accept their children's feelings about their siblings. He needs reassurance that it is OK to be angry with the baby and that you care about his feelings. Talk with him about what the baby does that makes him angry and about what he may do when he feels that way.

Page 24: *Is there something that we read about that you would like to try with (your baby's name)?* Your child will need your guidance and encouragement as she tries out new ways of playing and solving problems. Be sure to let her know how important her efforts are both to the baby and to the family.

KIDS CAN COOPERATE,
By Elizabeth Crary

Provides a practical approach to teaching children skills they need to solve problems themselves.

112 Pages, 8½ × 11, $7.95

WITHOUT SPANKING OR SPOILING
By Elizabeth Crary

A practical approach to toddler or preschool guidance. Combines a variety of child guidance techniques in one easy-to-use book.

102 Pages, 8 × 10, $7.95

IT'S MY BODY
By Lory Freeman

Offers children a strategy for dealing with uncomfortable touch whether it is tickling or more serious abuse.

32 Pages, 5½ × 8½, $3.00

Part of the **Children's Safety Series** available from
Parenting Press, Inc.

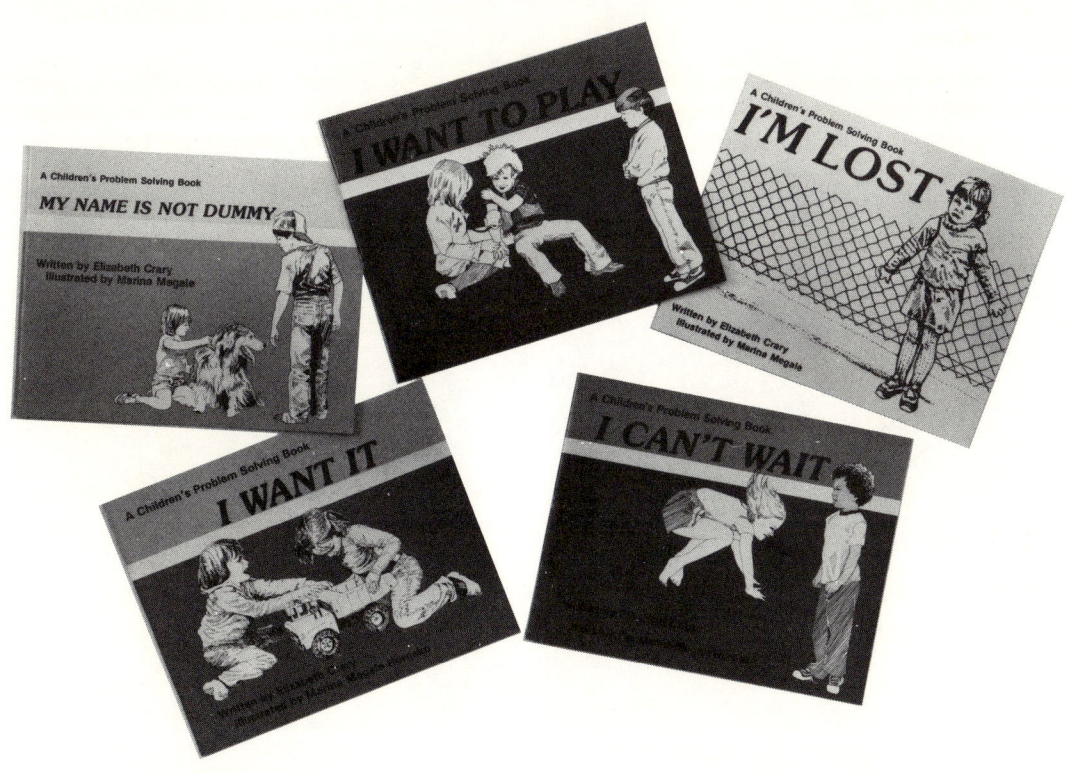

THE CHILDREN'S PROBLEM SOLVING SERIES
By Elizabeth Crary

Offers children a variety of alternatives and invites them to consider how their behavior affects others. Each book focuses on a different potential conflict. **I Want It** - possessions. **I Can't Wait** - issue of time. **I Want To Play** - how to find a friend. **My Name is Not Dummy** - issue of name calling and **I'm Lost** - what to do when lost.

32 Pages, 8 × 10, $3.95

See Your Bookseller Or Write

Parenting Press, Inc.
Suite 500, 7750 31st Ave NE, Seattle, WA 98115